Organizing Love in *Black Pearl*

History, memory, absence: how can we listen to the silenced names, the silencing betrayal of power, and the silence before it breaks? *Black Pearl* takes a searing, fearless look into the violence on the heart and construct of identity, and pushes "into the touch of things" to feel "our names inside" the rooted will that endures, the will that remembers, the will that loves.

Arisa White writes a kind of heroic resistance that sings contrapuntally, we do not forget intertwined histories and perspectives that are at the heart of a reign of brutality, we sing into the future the litany of dead names. We are led compassionately and fiercely, to organize a cosmological we.

– **Tsering Wangmo Dhompa**, author of numerous books, including *My Rice Tastes Like the Lake* (2011) and *A Home in Tibet* (2013)

Black Pearl

eight poems and a poetic drama
for four voices

Arisa White

NOMADIC PRESS

OAKLAND

111 FAIRMOUNT AVENUE
OAKLAND, CA 94611

BROOKLYN

475 KENT AVENUE #302
BROOKLYN, NY 11249

WWW.NOMADICPRESS.ORG

MASTHEAD

FOUNDING AND MANAGING EDITOR
J. K. FOWLER

ASSOCIATE EDITOR
MICHAELA MULLIN

DESIGN
J. K. FOWLER

MISSION STATEMENT

Nomadic Press is a 501 (C)(3) not-for-profit organization that supports the works of emerging and established writers and artists. Through publications (including translations) and performances, Nomadic Press aims to build community among artists and across disciplines.

SUBMISSIONS

Nomadic Press wholeheartedly accepts unsolicited book manuscripts. To submit your work, please visit www.nomadicpress.org/submissions

DISTRIBUTION

Orders by trade bookstores and wholesalers:
Small Press Distribution,
1341 Seventh Street
Berkeley, CA 94701
spd@spdbooks.org
(510) 524-1668 / (800) 869-7553

Black Pearl

This book was made possible by a loving community of chosen family and friends, old and new.

For author questions or to book a reading at your bookstore, university/school, or alternative establishment, please send an email to info@nomadicpress.org.

Cover artwork by Arthur Johnstone and Livien Yin; author portraits by Arthur Johnstone

Published by Nomadic Press, 111 Fairmount Avenue, Oakland, CA 94611

Fourth printing, 2020

Printed in the United States of America

LIBRARY OF CONGRESS CATALOGING-IN-PUBLICATION DATA

White, Arisa 1979 –
Title: *Black Pearl*
P. CM.
Summary: Love is alive in White's eight poems and poetic drama that call on the feminine presence, through ancestral memory and legacy, to heal a broken heart.

[1. POETRY/DEATH, GRIEF, LOSS. 3. POETRY/FAMILY. 3. AMERICAN GENERAL.] I. III. TITLE.

LIBRARY OF CONGRESS CONTROL NUMBER: 2016903544

ISBN: 978-0-9970933-1-5

Black Pearl

eight poems and a poetic drama
for four voices

Arisa White

NOMADIC
PRESS

Say Her name.

NACRE

1.

Everything is very different now—
your shape has failed me. I want to scream
you into a sacred geometric form. It hurts
in my memory—broken bones for a house and car
paid down, a debt I bought for love. These are things
we do for each other, be family in that manner
where thank-yous run scarce and birthday suited.
On the bruise end of your betrayals, I feel homeless
as the day I was born. What freedom was carved out
from her uncomfortable kiss? On the devil's clean five,
we are no better picking petals from a square rose. I don't
need your nots, your ripped dollar or Sacagawea coined
to a legacy of backsies, or your tail of turning away.

2.

We can stare at each other,
at that fork in the road, and if
we are rare, I'm not done bleeding.

We can take fruits before their time,
and leave the pits without burial—
what part do you want to play?

Your shoulders are cold, girlfriend.
The whiskey is rock-free—
you need to let down your terror.

We were good news, our hands were
so much ink and word after word,
I couldn't stop touching you.

In another's hair, you got tangled,
and in the direction of your heroics,
she stirred. Starts are always shining—

Clear the sky with my rewind and give
our backs the proper wings to get
caught up in a silver lining.

We can abracadabra through
our hang-ups and love ourselves
according to mountains and hoodoos.

3.

I look at an arm severed from its torso,
and I know it belongs to me because
the blood proves its sorrow. I've let myself go
distant and abroad and in my handwriting
postcards are written—is this what is left?
The body after breath. Grief after birds
have chosen the bush and not my apologies.
What new love will receive our candlelight?
Across this island body I toss salt and watch
the skin lift water, a sunset sweet as mango
is a muscle in the arm. We once held the sky
from falling. Although I have many strings,
none as beautiful as your violin. I will miss
your song on my boulevard, you seeing me
slender and reedy at the curtains. We now
know the difference between gods and ships.
I will not resemble trees and their reaching.
I'll favor night when bombs ignite elsewhere
or a decorative suffocation I cannot wear off
or a kiss in the brine of its narcissism or a ghost
too spook to look you square or a burning thing
like a country, like a woman brought to her knees.

4.

I woke in a sweat, on the verge of spilling into your arms,
lost in my terrifying scream you said released shivers.
We covered ourselves again in down. But to my left,
having abandoned the suite of my heart, a serpent
who disregarded the personal space I needed to keep
my security guarded, spoke in its own body language,
in a silence that coiled around my tongue and I didn't
say to you I was scared of your white lines and crying
wolves, your attention turned by shiny things—that you
dragged this Testament symbol to my bed. Were we wholly
Or animals we once were who couldn't welcome the anima
we are, because our breaks made us choose between air
or water when our fingers still needed to hymn our hertz.

5.

To take away this pain, I opened up,
and you took from me a chocolate.
To free us both from this autumn, I float
from the sea with refreshed pirouettes,
my jade a bit more spring, your face a torch
on the shore. The mighty feel of your crown
in my muscles, your fists burn deep in my eggs.
The sun takes out her breast and nurses the babies
to brown in her rays. Gone are my prayers
from your temples, the kites we believed.
Against the pull of your jawline, I chase
this old self to dust, and slip into my stars.

6.

Our house-beat don't bring the cops knocking.
No more apologetic sunflowers, dollar-store stationary
to color-code our fictions. I need Mary J. and Mary Jane
and not the blue that Pecola wanted—I have my blues
and blacks and these unsettled greens that shoot up to pin
when my rage reaches extreme Fahrenheits. To the rooftop
where "No more drama" shakes my shoulders, drops them
up and down like I can rid them of change, like I can take
a man for all he's worth, and my heels lift off the ground
and heels put me back to earth. Through my backbody
a tremble, a thunder, my clouds can't keep me prisoner
and I am patient as a kink that grows out this black skin
into a pea that refuses me pins-and-needles because this is
not the handiwork I come numb to do. To flatten under
a Sisyphus roll and into a bedlam of jelly mouths whose lo
is so waterfall I'm left at a single drop. No more in your
thirst, no more your city of diminishing oaks, I'm no more
your twenty four-sevens. No more in your heart, my applau

7.

The things to be grateful for are the trees
that hold this earth together. Their roots grab—
as we do with grass, a fistful of blades we pull
until they pull away and send us to land
on our backs. I'm not that kind of money
that makes this world thirsty. Not of its blood,
share not an idea fraternal—red is the color
of my tallies. For fear of being ashy, I keep
the company of coconuts and sheas, and I'm
caught in a ponderosa about how you must
lessen yourself to stack zeros in your banks.

8.

Hammers and Harriets will care for me, words from my mothers, and yes will
Lions and twins, greyhounds in the throats of my happy hours will
Senseis and bastards, dope beats and those who strip for rain
Fire starters and border crossers will—we who do not give a fuck will
The queer and new normal, and truth that splits your tongue
Verdant laughter will, hair wrapped into fists, revolutions will
Virgins from the rough, stuck-ups with their deuces
Surely cook-up love and the sparrows of Brooklyn's kingdom will
Orphans who gallop wild, train-wrecks who choke on trees
All navels made by innies, all innies made for outies, and they will
Lip lickers and goats and the will they rode in on, a ghost-sung serenade,
the capitalized will, a will of sell-outs, a will of Oreos, a will fresh off the boat,
this heart that be my will—this thigh, this birdie will, this busted quartet
She who reminds me of my limitations, She who lets me be limitless
Tall drinks of halos will, farewells to take will, and wet wounds will flaunt their light.

BLACK PEARL

a poetic drama for four voices

Voices

Narrator
You
Driver
Deejay

Time

Your darkest hour

Setting

A crossroads where a street meets an avenue

Here you have fallen to a ground unfamiliar with
your stomp, your corners and your beefs, no body is
calling your name—a mispronounced anomaly. Too
blur to be understood, you are where the ground done
shake, done burn, done sink into itself to show you
Her insides—a cave for all our birthings, a pitch
black wonder, a solemn O.

Oh

oh the silence it volumes tunnels into the O of your
canals, into an Oh off your drum, out of an O of your
breath, out of the Oh of your mouth, washed from the
O of your teardrop

Drops

drops you here in this place. A water rough goes
through you. Here in this place, on your knees,
knocking on this earth to call your people's music
into your bones, their laughter with no syntax, loose
and fresh their tongues, all them rhythms to heal.
Your heart thirsty for love is but a cup compared
to your body. Here, east of your spine, the ocean, a
conjunction in your story; the ocean, filled with vows
and hunger, and here you are—

Waiting

for a Black Pearl Taxicab
to take you to the Lake,
jeweled with lights
the City keeps running.

forgotten in your circuitry
remembered after the fact
the fact that is
twenty-four and seven years
I am hours
I am fumes
these pieces you rather not puzzle
10,000 portraits of dust
small confessions r.i.p. my palm—

Black Pearl pulls up before you On the radio, the deejay says, Dedicated to the children, women and men, to them all who died at the hands of loveless hearts, apathetic laws, became bricks in blue walls, and called back too soon—our plots cannot contain the sour.

A litany of dead names is said and remains in the atmosphere as a veil of sound.

I am not a star
I am missed and ancient
I am not heard
I am not blue eyes
I live these pages turning wild
I am not recognized

The backseat door opens before you can apply your pull. Driver greets you with obsidian eyes. Her dreadlocks, silver as a full moon, fall to her

elbows. She speaks like a chorus of
ancestors drives her lungs, I got you.

I am saying, where is the love?
I am saying, I'm the promise to hold
I am saying, how many rounds of names
must pass through my throat?

You clear the tears from your eyes.
Driver asks, Where you want to go?
You say, Take me home.

Driver keeps her eyes on the road,
her hands at 3 and 9, and all of her
sees you as a true spark. She holds you
in a body gaze—you've forgotten
such a communicating touch and
remember again the language of your
own presence. Speech happens with
lips parted or in silence. She meets
your eyes in the rearview, and the
ancestors declare,

The dirt is
where the bloom
comes from the buried

All these sheeps want to sleep me, *you say*

Before and unborn
our mothers carry
blood that brought us alive

push shush on my lips—shush me, *you say*

Her tears echo in US
like a canyon speak back to us
You've forgotten your voice made grand

silent to myself, silence builds me, *you say*

These crooked rooms,
not meant for standing,
let them tumble and fall

On the earth's door, you raised
your fist full of want, knocking
for an answer, knocking

master-tools be the house that house me, *you say*

And the ancestors want to know:
Why you knocking for?

I want these bricks out the walls of we, *you say*

Your fist full of thunder, knocking
for a beat to lay a rhyme, knocking

out from beneath His missionary hide, *you say*

And the ancestors want to know:
What you knocking for?

set free my tender-headed kitchen, *you say*

Your fist full of vex, knocking
for an angel to flex, knocking

cross my wounds with love, *you say*

The ancestors want to know,

What's all this killing for?

The deejay says the litany of dead names like the veil of sound lifted and the ocean took over his tongue and names come to the shore salted and ready for land.

My body I fear to swim,
    fear disconnects my line:
white noise has become the ghost of me,
    I hear myself haunt the dead silence
deaf and dead in this rift, a spook, a little am I.
    no continuity to dream of. No peep to my bac
no peep to eye. Alone and alienated in a construc
    they call me black

loud
wild
intimidating
too fresh
Bland
and my red is spilled all over

dirty
soucouyant
monkey
bitch
too Proud
by news so splitting it herds

You and Driver sync into a rhythm,
your words share the same root, be of
the same mother, act contrapuntally.

I've been called

three-fifths regarded
angry inhumanely
disadvantaged by people
nigger fashioned
Brown by colonizer's colors
capitalizing off our beads

You keep your fingers butterfly on
your chest like your heart is the vinyl
you're not allowed to touch.

This violence
on the heart
skips on "Nobody"
"Bumbaclot" "Ugly"
and their kin
cuts through
my veins.

Who you knocking for? *is the bridge that Driver lays into*
your grooves.

You look at the passing lights, the
night, the stillness as prayer atop these
roofs, the sky in shades of navy and
ash, and you can taste the silence
before it breaks,

Mothers, Mae I, Rae I, Pearl,
Esther, Gail. Mothers, May I, Margaret,
Carol, Elsie, Carol, Mariana, and Madeline,
and Mable. Mothers, Mae I, Rae I, Anna B, Jean,
Josephine, Ethel, Karla, and Lucinda, Jo. Mothers,
May I, Eleanor, Pat, Barbara, Ruby, Judy, Karen.
Mothers, Mae I, Rae I, Florette, GrandMother Rose :
who I knock for.

Driver stops Black Pearl near a
curbside garden and your door opens,

Take from your mother's garden
A pistil to put in your braids—

And you take a blossom that looks
like a trumpet of wind and Indian gold
and you wear it like a Holiday.

Sweet reminder to keep Her blessings
when beneath the spell of sorrow

You return to Black Pearl and Driver
resumes the engine's purr, and her
words,

Pick and eat Her yams and yucca,
Swiss chard and snap peas—

Your mother's garden isn't all peach.
What you take, you can't mistake

There's not a strange fruit
and forbidden is for pussies—

the reason they try to shut this mother down

You bring them to the up, to the air
to breathe,

Mothers, Mae I, Rae I, Pearl,
Esther, Gail. Mothers, May I, Margaret,
Carol, Elsie, Carol, Mariana, and Madeline,
and Mable. Mothers, Mae I, Rae I, Anna B, Jean,
Josephine, Ethel, Karla, and Lucinda, Jo. Mothers,
May I, Eleanor, Pat, Barbara, Ruby, Judy, Karen.
Mothers, Mae I, Rae I, Florette, GrandMother Rose,
who I knock for.

Driver drives Black Pearl to an
oak that fell when a storm rolled
through and now its roots starburst
from the dirt. Overlooking the Lake,
Black Pearl is put in park and Driver
turns her obsidian eyes on you,

There is no peace in running the truth of you,
no justice in naming your inheritance shatter,

all have trembled in your mask, but you are found
In your lagoons and liminal paradises, a tree grown

from the menses the baobab drank—
it's diameter the weeks in a year, it's bark generous,

around its circumference women on their hunches,
evenly spaced in preparation for flight

Your knocking resounds, spreads before your heart's pride,
roaring, roaring right from all these mouths of mater

GrandMother Rose is who I knock for.

The door opens again, and you hold
your grandmother's name in your
mouth like hard candy.

Rise yourself to enter roots,
framed as a doorway, as a window,

the height for you to passage through

You rise through her name, Rose
you grow yourself to standing,

from the ground no longer fallen,
Rose

The deejay plays some keys of life and tells you about your
Rose Carter, your Geechee parts, from when your people were
down South,

Petals and thorns
grit and perseverance
ego soothed by your knees'
arthritic crunch—you getting up,
to the deep side, where
roots reach, where
Rose rose from
Her red clay sleep,

Boo creeping in just
when the moon
makes Her descent,
when Rose smelled
that same toilette
water from another
toilet piece of ass,
and when Boo pulled
them sheets to see
a shotgun, Rose said,
This's who *I'm* fuckin wit.

You say, Never knew GrandMother Rose
had that kind of bitch and spice.

*You reach your hand to the roots of
this oak, more old than old, and
you feel its memory. The roots reach
back to you and Driver remarks on
where you stand,*

Here, your shadow retires. Put to rest your restless, enter into the touch of things, what the body senses. You must look by listening to free you from the power of what them say. Feel our names inside. That core of you is the core of you is the core we're rooting for. Here, is the will to endure.

*Driver meets you at your side, brings
you into an embrace that makes you
feel the goodness inside. She points
her finger to the crescent above, the
grass, the skin of the Lake, then here,
and then there, until her finger has*

made a constellation of life and things
and all things being. Her palm rests
at the back of your heart, and when
her hand returns to her hip, the heat it
leaves, melts your ice. The water is
filled with Driver's voice,

Without Her, you
have no body to feel
to feel the feel
to know the feel
to swear on the feel—
it's mighty real

In Her body, your
body, the sweet preverb
quiet, the sea untranslated
body is Her
body is a body
of unimaginable real
where what we call
magic is dark depths
where no Sankofa reach
in the woe
in the wonder
in the wick
that stands to burn
for your body

give Her praise
up high, your palms
contralto, you bear
Her note, surviving
in our words

Ma
Ma
Ma
Ma
arrives from all our fragments
and steps foot here

Where you from?
You stand more strong, more sure,
From here.

Driver sits down on the grass, with its blades long and glowing. With a pound on the ground, she invites you to sit next to her. Driver gives you a moment to abide, and you do, and she lets her 'locks flow down one shoulder. She holds your hand, while she drops this knowledge,

When it does not suffice that you are USAmerican,
that you must be somewhere not BedfordStuyvesant,
it is that rebel pearl-diver blood that makes this skin other than what is expected. Is it Negra Azalea, Venezuelan born, beneath shade of trees that scream their hurt when roots are torn, the Isle of Las Tetas de Dolores. Her, the woman who planted it all, our freedom seeded. She's the tierra that features most.

Who am I?

That depth of sea survived . . .
When I say ship, I mean the one from Dutch—
Prima Madre in its belly, learning ways she is peri-

carp around a seed. Azalea in her belly, put there
by a dull and fiery face, on an afternoon, rape
joined our helixes. Her tongue held on to No.
When I say ship, I mean Prima was. Shipped
then shipped, she didn't know where she was.

She wanted for her daughter swimming ways.
Cape Verde, her island, taught her so.
Prima slaved for pearls. Carried down
into feet by boulders, Prima's body greased,
a slick allegiance to finding Negra Paca's black pearl—
in a league she couldn't quite descend, in the mouth
of a ladena named Paca was Prima's freedom. The pearl
the size of your eye, and many lost sight to getting it.

What emerged from Prima's darkest deep
wasn't the jewel of another's suffering, but home
she tasted too frequently in these waters. She blacked out,
gave up her air for the drink of it, and rested on oyster
beds.

Where am I bound?

Azalea motherless, and the magic of never
been born a child, she was a sure profit.
She had a talent for holding breath, fainted
never, not a shark touch her, like a dolphin,
her body with no death in it, ode and spring to sea.

She was able to find the pearl on a full-moon night.
In a dream, Prima came to her, and Azalea followed
her mother to the sea. There, glowing in the low tide,
a trinity of albino stingrays that led her to where Paca
drowned. The black pearl steady in her mouth.

Where do I come from?

Azalea's lips,
that kiss,
to Paca's mouth.

Driver opens her hand, and there, balanced on her lifeline is the black pearl. You wonder, Is this for me, and Driver answers back with, Yes and a Yes, some more. You smile, feeling happiness like a friend you haven't seen since elementary, and gratitude reveals its source.

On the radio, the deejay stirs the litany of dead names into a house-beat, into an indigo pulse, into the joy we summons to gift our dead.

You are awoken,
we see you through

Love you strong,
these blues make violets
with your redbone

We walk the path,
the paths you walk,
our feet the meters
your talk come through

Through us, you are alive,
no lie can tell about you

You respond to the melody with all the choreography carried in your bones. You abandon your shame and let your limbs celebrate: Wops and Running Mans, Pepper Seeds and Whines and the madras your hands sign.

You are awoken,
your shells, you shed
to know truth

For you, our tears, our kinks,
our how-we-do, our milk,
yams, our breaths, little
deaths, these mending needles,
roots and rivers, what we do with rue

Your blood a hive, oh honey,
sweet your pulse brings you close to being
Your heart is unblinking
Your spirit wolf

You are awoken,
a cosmological we,
infinite pearl—you are precious.
So it be, your back, we at,
we got you.

The litany of dead names becomes a murmuration of swallow. The veil of sound is more like crisp, the first bite into, like honey on a spoon to gild your song, like the bling of a ray served to break your fast.

Driver and you sit watching east and
you notice how the Lake rises and fall,
and you notice, too, the swell in you.
When the embankments go
invisible, you feel its stillness
convincing you to walk across
it. The morning is yellow in you and

Driver's eyes, and you have something to say,

I am here in it, in love
with the for-sense to whole
myself whole again.
Love is its own enough
as its own presence—
I've been labored here.
The people I love are in it,
and we breathe to attest
our love is for certain.

Driver ponytails her 'locks, and they fountain from her crown,

ou are sharp for the real,
our breaks give you an edge
oud out comes your laughter, it raises the roof
our anger is an organizing sound

Driver walks back to Black Pearl, and begins to warm the engine. You return to the backseat and Driver continues with sense,

iot against the guards—civil is a judgment
our beauty is a truth that doesn't crack—take the flags down!
our inhale removes the robes off this eroding empire—
e behind the trees to where your hands made a beat:
u're a river, that sweet fresh, a breath of first take.

Driver goes in the direction of home, down First Avenue. She turns

the volume up, and the deejay
says the litany of dead names like they
are dressed to the nines in red silk,
fashioned from rainbows whose arrows
call us into a familiar and safe high,
and your skin shines. When the names
turn into aerosols, you put the black
pearl in your mouth, and savor these
three words,

I
L-O-V-E
You

I
L-O-V-E
You

I
L-O-V-E
You

I
L-O-V-E
You

I
L-O-V-E
You

I
L-O-V-E
You

I
L O V E
You.

NOTES

Poem "6" makes reference to the Mary J. Blige song "No More Drama," from her 2001 album of the same title and to Toni Morrison's main character, Pecola, in the 1970 novel *The Bluest Eye*. Pecola desired blue eyes because she thought they would make her more loveable and acceptable.

In the poetic drama, *Black Pearl*, Bland, Proud, and Brown refers to Sandra Bland, Penny Proud, and Michael Brown, all of whom were killed by police in 2015.

ACKNOWLEDGEMENTS

Thank you to J. K. Fowler and Nomadic Press for publishing this work; Derek Lassiter, Tammy L. Hall, and Amber McZeal for bringing your voices and vision to *Black Pearl*; Eli Renaud for taking the time to be a reader; and to Tsering Wango Dhompa and Leora Fridman for offering your praise. Thank you.

ARISA WHITE is a Cave Canem fellow and her most recent poetry collection *You're the Most Beautiful Thing That Happened* was nominated for a Lambda Literary Award. She is the co-author of *Biddy Mason Speaks Up*, the second book in the Fighting for Justice series for young readers. Her poetic hybrid collection *Who's Your Daddy?* is forthcoming from Augury Books in 2021. She is an assistant professor of creative writing at Colby College. arisawhite.com